HOW TO BUILD AND RUN A REFINERY

- A Comprehensive Guide

By

MAXWELL OKEGBE

HOW TO BUILD AND RUN A REFINERY

CONTENTS

Page

Chapter 1 - Introduction   7

Brief overview of the oil and gas industry

Why refineries are important in the industry

The purpose of the book and its target audience

The benefits of building and running a refinery

Chapter 2 - Planning and Design   16

Factors to consider when planning a refinery

Environmental impact assessment and regulatory requirements

Types of refineries and their functions

Basic refinery design and layout

Process flow diagram and equipment selection

Safety and security considerations

Chapter 3 - Construction and Commissioning 40

Site preparation and grading

Construction of foundations, storage tanks, and pipelines

Installation of process equipment and instrumentation

Electrical and control systems

Testing and commissioning of the refinery

Chapter 4 - Operation and Maintenance 60

Start-up procedures and initial operations

Operating the refinery efficiently and safely

Monitoring and controlling refinery processes

Troubleshooting and problem-solving

Preventive and predictive maintenance

Emergency response procedures

Chapter 8 - Conclusion   *128*

Chapter 1

INTRODUCTION

The oil and gas industry is one of the most important industries in the world, powering transportation, heating, and electricity generation. Within the industry, refineries play a critical role in converting crude oil into usable products such as gasoline, diesel, and jet fuel.

This book is designed to provide a comprehensive guide on building and running a refinery, from planning and design to operation and maintenance. It is intended for engineers, project managers, investors, and other professionals interested in the refining industry.

Building and running a refinery can be a complex and challenging process, but it can also be highly rewarding. Refineries can generate significant revenue and provide stable employment for local communities. In addition, refineries are essential for ensuring a reliable supply of fuel and other products.

This book will cover the basics of refinery planning and design, construction and commissioning, operation and maintenance, product quality and distribution, economics and finance, and future trends and developments. By the end of this book, readers should have a solid understanding of the refinery building process and be better equipped to make informed decisions regarding refinery projects.

BRIEF OVERVIEW OF THE OIL AND GAS INDUSTRY

The oil and gas industry is a global industry that involves the exploration, extraction, refining, and distribution of petroleum products. It is a vital industry that powers transportation, heating, and electricity generation, and plays a critical role in the global economy.

The industry is made up of a range of companies, including major international oil companies, national oil companies, independent oil and gas companies, and service providers. These companies operate across the entire oil and gas value chain, from exploration and production to refining and distribution.

The industry is characterized by a high degree of technology, innovation, and collaboration. Advances in technology have led to increased efficiency in exploration and production, improved refining processes, and more environmentally friendly operations.

The oil and gas industry is subject to a range of economic, political, and environmental factors that can affect supply and demand. This includes changes in global oil prices, geopolitical tensions, and concerns about climate change and greenhouse gas emissions.

Overall, the oil and gas industry is a critical component of the global economy, providing essential energy resources to power economic growth and development.

WHY REFINERIES ARE IMPORTANT IN THE INDUSTRY

Refineries are important in the oil and gas industry because they are responsible for converting crude oil into a range of useful products, including gasoline, diesel, jet fuel, and heating oil. Crude oil in its raw form is not useful and needs to be processed before it can be used as a fuel or in other applications.

Without refineries, the oil and gas industry would not be able to meet the demand for the products that it produces. Refineries play a critical role in ensuring that there is a steady supply of fuels and other products that are essential for transportation, heating, and other purposes.

Refineries also add value to crude oil by producing higher-value products from a lower-value feedstock. This can increase the profitability of the industry and provide economic benefits to communities that host refineries.

In addition, refineries are subject to strict safety and environmental regulations, which ensure that they operate in a safe and responsible manner. This helps to minimize the impact of the oil and gas industry on the environment and protect the health and safety of workers and nearby communities.

Overall, refineries are a critical component of the oil and gas industry, ensuring that there is a reliable supply of fuel and other products that are essential for modern life.

THE PURPOSE OF THE BOOK AND ITS TARGET AUDIENCE

The purpose of this book is to provide a comprehensive guide on building and running a refinery, covering the entire process from planning and design to operation and maintenance. The book is intended for engineers, project managers, investors, and other professionals interested in the refining industry.

The book aims to provide a detailed overview of the key considerations and challenges involved in building and running a refinery. It will cover a range of topics, including refinery planning and design, construction and commissioning, operation and maintenance, product quality and distribution, economics and finance, and future trends and developments.

The target audience for this book includes:

Engineers and technical professionals involved in the design, construction, and operation of refineries.

Project managers responsible for overseeing refinery projects, from planning to execution.

Investors and financiers interested in investing in refinery projects.

Regulators and policy-makers involved in the oversight and regulation of the refining industry.

Students and researchers interested in the oil and gas industry and the role of refineries within it.

Overall, this book is intended to provide a comprehensive resource for anyone interested in the refining industry, from those just starting out to experienced professionals looking to deepen their knowledge and understanding of the industry.

The benefits of building and running a refinery

Building and running a refinery can offer a range of benefits, including:

Economic benefits: Refineries can generate significant revenue for the companies that own and operate them, as well as provide stable employment for local communities. Refineries can also provide economic benefits to the wider region, such as increased tax revenue and support for local businesses.

Energy security: Refineries play a critical role in ensuring a reliable supply of fuel and other petroleum products. By producing these products domestically, countries can reduce their reliance on imported energy resources and increase their energy security.

Value-added processing: Refineries can add value to crude oil by producing higher-value products from a lower-value feedstock. This can increase the profitability of the oil and gas industry and provide economic benefits to communities that host refineries.

Environmental benefits: Refineries are subject to strict safety and environmental regulations, which ensure that they operate in a safe and responsible manner. This helps to minimize the impact of the oil and gas industry on the environment and protect the health and safety of workers and nearby communities.

Innovation and technology development: The refining industry is characterized by a high degree of technology and innovation. Building and running a refinery can provide opportunities for companies to develop new technologies and processes that can increase efficiency, reduce costs, and improve environmental performance.

Overall, building and running a refinery can offer a range of benefits, from economic growth and energy security to environmental protection and technological innovation. However, it is important to recognize that building and running a refinery can also come with challenges and risks, which will be addressed in this book.

Chapter 2

PLANNING AND DESIGN

B uilding a refinery requires careful planning and design to ensure that the facility is safe, efficient, and cost-effective. This chapter will cover the key considerations and steps involved in the planning and design of a refinery.

2.1 REFINERY LOCATION

The location of a refinery is a critical consideration, as it can affect the cost of construction, transportation, and distribution. Factors to consider when selecting a location include proximity to crude oil sources, access to transportation infrastructure, availability of water and utilities, and environmental and regulatory considerations.

2.2 REFINERY CONFIGURATION

The configuration of a refinery refers to the types of processing units that are used and how they are arranged. Refinery configurations can vary widely depending on the feedstock, product mix, and other factors. Common processing units include crude distillation units, catalytic cracking units, hydrotreating units, and reforming units.

2.3 FEEDSTOCK SELECTION

The selection of feedstock is another critical consideration in the planning and design of a refinery. The choice of feedstock can affect the product mix and the efficiency of the refinery. Factors to consider when selecting a feedstock include the quality and quantity of the crude oil, the sulfur content, and the availability of other types of feedstock.

2.4 PROCESS FLOW DIAGRAM

The process flow diagram is a schematic representation of the processing units and equipment that make up the refinery. It provides a visual representation of the flow of materials and energy through the facility and can be used to identify potential bottlenecks and areas for optimization.

2.5 EQUIPMENT SELECTION

The selection of equipment is a key consideration in the design of a refinery. Equipment must be selected based on the processing requirements, the feedstock characteristics, and the desired product mix. Equipment must also be selected with safety and environmental considerations in mind.

2.6 SAFETY AND ENVIRONMENTAL CONSIDERATIONS

Safety and environmental considerations are critical in the planning and design of a refinery. Refineries are subject to strict safety and environmental regulations, which require the implementation of safety and environmental management systems. These systems must be designed to minimize the risk of accidents and to mitigate the environmental impact of refinery operations.

2.7 Cost estimation

Cost estimation is an important consideration in the planning and design of a refinery. The cost of building and operating a refinery can be significant, and accurate cost estimates are necessary to ensure that the project is financially viable. Factors to consider when estimating costs include the cost of materials, labor, equipment, and regulatory compliance.

2.8 Project management

Effective project management is essential in the planning and design of a refinery. Project management involves coordinating the activities of the various stakeholders involved in the project, from engineers and contractors to regulators and investors. Effective project management can help to ensure that the project is completed on time, within budget, and to the required standards.

In conclusion, planning and design are critical steps in building a refinery. The location, configuration, feedstock selection, process flow diagram, equipment selection, safety and environmental considerations, cost estimation, and project management are all important factors to consider in the planning and design process. A well-designed refinery can provide economic benefits, energy security, value-added processing, environmental protection, and technological innovation.

FACTORS TO CONSIDER WHEN PLANNING A REFINERY

When planning a refinery, there are several key factors to consider, including:

LOCATION

The location of the refinery is a critical consideration, as it can impact the cost of construction, transportation, and distribution. Factors to consider when selecting a location include proximity to crude oil sources, access to transportation infrastructure, availability of water and utilities, and environmental and regulatory considerations.

Feedstock selection

The selection of feedstock is another critical consideration in the planning and design of a refinery. The choice of feedstock can affect the product mix and the efficiency of the refinery. Factors to consider when selecting a feedstock include the quality and quantity of the crude oil, the sulfur content, and the availability of other types of feedstock.

Refinery configuration

The configuration of the refinery refers to the types of processing units that are used and how they are arranged. Refinery configurations can vary widely depending on the feedstock, product mix, and other factors. Common processing units include crude distillation units, catalytic cracking units, hydrotreating units, and reforming units.

Product mix

The product mix is another critical consideration when planning a refinery. The product mix can affect the profitability of the refinery, as some products may have higher margins than others. Factors to consider when selecting a product mix include market demand, product specifications, and regulatory requirements.

Environmental and safety considerations

Refineries are subject to strict safety and environmental regulations, which require the implementation of safety and environmental management systems. These systems must be designed to minimize the risk of accidents and to mitigate the environmental impact of refinery operations. Factors to consider include emissions, waste disposal, and emergency response planning.

Cost estimation

Cost estimation is an important consideration in the planning and design of a refinery. The cost of building and operating a refinery can be significant, and accurate cost estimates are necessary to ensure that the project is financially viable. Factors to consider when estimating costs include the cost of materials, labor, equipment, and regulatory compliance.

PROJECT MANAGEMENT

Effective project management is essential in the planning and design of a refinery. Project management involves coordinating the activities of the various stakeholders involved in the project, from engineers and contractors to regulators and investors. Effective project management can help to ensure that the project is completed on time, within budget, and to the required standards.

In conclusion, careful consideration of these factors is critical in the planning and design of a refinery. A well-designed refinery can provide economic benefits, energy security, value-added processing, environmental protection, and technological innovation.

Environmental impact assessment and regulatory requirements

Environmental impact assessment (EIA) is an important aspect of the planning and design of a refinery. An EIA is a study of the potential environmental effects of a proposed project, including its impact on air and water quality, soil, and wildlife. The purpose of an EIA is to identify potential environmental impacts and to develop measures to mitigate those impacts.

Regulatory requirements are another important consideration when planning a refinery. Refineries are subject to a wide range of federal, state, and local environmental regulations, including the Clean Air Act, the Clean Water Act, and the Resource Conservation and Recovery Act. These regulations are designed to protect the environment and human health by controlling emissions, preventing spills, and ensuring the safe handling and disposal of hazardous materials.

In order to comply with these regulations, refineries must develop and implement a range of environmental management plans and procedures. These may include:

Air pollution control plans: Refineries must control emissions of pollutants such as sulfur dioxide, nitrogen oxides, particulate matter, and volatile organic compounds. Air pollution control plans may include the use of emissions controls, such as scrubbers, catalytic converters, and flue gas desulfurization systems.

Spill prevention, control, and countermeasures plans: Refineries must develop plans to prevent, control, and respond to spills of oil and other hazardous materials. These plans may include measures such as containment systems, spill response teams, and emergency response plans.

Waste management plans: Refineries generate a wide range of hazardous and non-hazardous waste streams. Waste management plans must be developed to ensure that these wastes are properly handled, stored, and disposed of in accordance with regulatory requirements.

Water pollution control plans: Refineries must control the discharge of pollutants into surface waters and groundwater. Water pollution control plans may include measures such as wastewater treatment systems, stormwater management systems, and groundwater monitoring programs.

In conclusion, compliance with environmental regulations is critical for the successful operation of a refinery. Effective environmental management plans and procedures can help to ensure that the refinery operates in a safe and environmentally responsible manner.

TYPES OF REFINERIES AND THEIR FUNCTIONS

There are several types of refineries, each designed to process a specific type of crude oil and produce specific types of petroleum products. The main types of refineries include:

Topping refinery: A topping refinery is the simplest type of refinery and is designed to process only the lightest crude oil fractions. These refineries typically produce gasoline, kerosene, and diesel fuel.

HYDROSKIMMING REFINERY

A hydroskimming refinery is designed to process medium to heavy crude oil fractions. These refineries use a process called hydrotreating to remove sulfur, nitrogen, and other impurities from the crude oil. They typically produce gasoline, kerosene, diesel fuel, and heating oil.

CONVERSION REFINERY

A conversion refinery is designed to convert heavy crude oil fractions into lighter, more valuable products through a variety of processes, including cracking, coking, and reforming. These refineries typically produce gasoline, diesel fuel, jet fuel, and petrochemical feedstocks.

COMPLEX REFINERY

A complex refinery is a combination of a hydroskimming refinery and a conversion refinery. These refineries are designed to process a wide range of crude oil types and produce a broad range of products, including gasoline, diesel fuel, jet fuel, and petrochemical feedstocks.

THE MAIN FUNCTIONS OF A REFINERY ARE:-

SEPARATION

The primary function of a refinery is to separate crude oil into its various components, including gasoline, diesel fuel, and other products.

CONVERSION

Refineries use a variety of processes to convert heavy crude oil fractions into lighter, more valuable products, such as gasoline and diesel fuel.

PURIFICATION

Refineries remove impurities from the crude oil and the refined products through a variety of processes, including hydrotreating and catalytic cracking.

BLENDING

Refineries blend different products together to create specific grades of gasoline, diesel fuel, and other products.

STORAGE AND DISTRIBUTION

Refineries store the finished products in tanks and distribute them to customers through pipelines, trucks, and other means of transportation.

In conclusion, the type of refinery and its function depend on the type of crude oil being processed and the desired end products. The main functions of a refinery are separation, conversion, purification, blending, and storage and distribution.

BASIC REFINERY DESIGN AND LAYOUT

The basic design and layout of a refinery may vary depending on its size, capacity, and the types of crude oil and products it processes. However, most refineries follow a similar basic design and layout.

CRUDE OIL STORAGE AND HANDLING

Crude oil is typically delivered to the refinery by pipeline, tanker, or railcar and is stored in large tanks before being processed. The storage tanks are often located near the processing units for ease of access.

DISTILLATION UNIT

The first processing unit in the refinery is the distillation unit, which separates the crude oil into different components based on their boiling points. The lighter components, such as gasoline and propane, are typically produced at the top of the distillation tower, while heavier components, such as diesel fuel and heating oil, are produced at the bottom.

CONVERSION UNIT

The conversion unit uses various processes, such as cracking, coking, and reforming, to convert heavy components into lighter, more valuable products. The conversion unit typically includes several processing units, including a fluid catalytic cracker (FCC), a hydrocracker, and a coker.

TREATMENT UNIT

The treatment unit removes impurities, such as sulfur, nitrogen, and metals, from the crude oil and refined products. The treatment unit typically includes several processing units, including a hydrotreater, a desulfurization unit, and a hydrofiner.

BLENDING AND STORAGE

The final products from the refinery are blended to meet specific product specifications, such as octane rating for gasoline. The blended products are stored in large tanks before being shipped to customers.

The layout of a refinery is often organized around a central processing area, where the distillation, conversion, and treatment units are located. The processing units are typically interconnected by pipelines and are often arranged in a linear or circular layout to minimize the distance between the units. The storage tanks and loading facilities are typically located near the processing units for ease of access.

In conclusion, the basic design and layout of a refinery includes crude oil storage and handling, a distillation unit, a conversion unit, a treatment unit, and blending and storage facilities. The layout is often organized around a central processing area with interconnected processing units and storage tanks located nearby.

Process flow diagram and equipment selection

Process flow diagrams (PFDs) are important documents that show the sequence of processes and the equipment used in a refinery. A PFD typically includes the following information:

The process flow: The process flow is shown through a series of interconnected boxes and arrows that illustrate the sequence of processes.

Equipment used: The equipment used in each process is shown in the corresponding box.

Process conditions: The temperature, pressure, and other conditions required for each process are typically shown on the PFD.

Product outputs: The products produced at each stage of the process are typically shown on the PFD.

Equipment selection is an important part of refinery design. The equipment used in a refinery depends on the type of crude oil being processed, the products being produced, and the desired production capacity. Some common types of equipment used in refineries include:

Distillation towers: Distillation towers are used to separate crude oil into its various components based on their boiling points.

Cracking units: Cracking units are used to break down heavy hydrocarbons into lighter components.

Hydrotreaters: Hydrotreaters are used to remove sulfur and other impurities from refined products.

Catalytic converters: Catalytic converters are used to convert hydrocarbons into more valuable products, such as gasoline.

Storage tanks: Storage tanks are used to store crude oil and refined products before they are shipped to customers.

Pumps and compressors: Pumps and compressors are used to move crude oil and refined products through the refinery.

Heat exchangers: Heat exchangers are used to transfer heat from one fluid to another in order to maintain the desired process conditions.

When selecting equipment for a refinery, it is important to consider factors such as reliability, efficiency, safety, and cost. The equipment must be able to handle the volume and type of crude oil being processed and must be designed to meet the environmental and regulatory requirements of the refinery.

In conclusion, process flow diagrams and equipment selection are important aspects of refinery design. The PFDs show the sequence of processes and the equipment used in a refinery, while equipment selection is based on the type of crude oil being processed, the products being produced, and the desired production capacity. It is important to consider factors such as reliability, efficiency, safety, and cost when selecting equipment for a refinery.

SAFETY AND SECURITY CONSIDERATIONS

Safety and security considerations are critical when building and running a refinery. The refining process involves handling and processing flammable, explosive, and toxic materials, making it a potentially hazardous industry. Safety and security measures are put in place to prevent accidents, protect personnel and equipment, and minimize the impact of any incidents that may occur. Some important safety and security considerations for a refinery include:

Process safety management: Process safety management (PSM) is a systematic approach to managing the hazards associated with processes that involve highly hazardous chemicals. PSM programs typically include hazard assessments, operating procedures, employee training, and emergency response plans.

Equipment design and maintenance: Equipment used in a refinery must be designed, constructed, and maintained to ensure safe operation. This includes regular inspection, testing, and repair of equipment to identify and address potential safety hazards.

Emergency response planning: Refineries must have well-developed emergency response plans in place to address potential incidents, including fires, explosions, chemical releases, and natural disasters. These plans should include procedures for notifying emergency responders, evacuating personnel, and implementing response actions.

Physical security: Refineries must be physically secure to prevent unauthorized access to the site and protect personnel and equipment from intentional harm. This may include fencing, access control systems, surveillance cameras, and security personnel.

Cybersecurity: Refineries are increasingly vulnerable to cyber-attacks, which can result in disruption of operations, theft of intellectual property, and compromise of sensitive information.

Refineries must have strong cybersecurity measures in place to protect their computer systems and networks from cyber threats.

Environmental considerations:

Refineries must comply with environmental regulations to minimize the impact of their operations on air, water, and soil quality. This may include measures to reduce emissions, monitor and control wastewater discharges, and manage hazardous waste.

In conclusion, safety and security considerations are critical when building and running a refinery. Refineries must implement processes to manage the hazards associated with their operations, maintain equipment to ensure safe operation, develop emergency response plans, and implement physical and cybersecurity measures. They must also comply with environmental regulations to minimize the impact of their operations on the environment.

Chapter 3

CONSTRUCTION AND COMMISSIONING

C onstruction and commissioning are important stages in the development of a refinery. In this chapter, we will discuss the key considerations for the construction and commissioning of a refinery.

CONSTRUCTION

Construction is the process of building the refinery. During this stage, the site is prepared, the equipment is installed, and the necessary infrastructure is built. Some key considerations during the construction phase include:

Project management: The construction phase requires careful project management to ensure that the project is completed on time and within budget. This includes planning, scheduling, and coordination of contractors and suppliers.

Health and safety: Construction sites can be hazardous, so it is important to prioritize health and safety. This includes implementing safety procedures, providing appropriate personal protective equipment, and training workers on safety practices.

Quality control: Quality control measures are important to ensure that the refinery is built to the required specifications. This includes inspecting equipment, testing materials, and ensuring that work is carried out to the required standards.

Commissioning

Commissioning is the process of bringing the refinery into operation. This involves testing the equipment, ensuring that it is working as intended, and making any necessary adjustments. Some key considerations during the commissioning phase include:

Start-up procedures: The start-up procedures for a refinery are critical to ensure that the equipment operates correctly and safely. This includes starting up the equipment in the correct sequence, monitoring equipment performance, and making any necessary adjustments.

Operational testing: Operational testing is important to ensure that the equipment is working as intended. This includes testing the various processes, measuring the performance of the equipment, and identifying any areas that need to be improved.

Training: Staff training is critical to ensure that personnel can operate the equipment safely and effectively. This includes training on the operation of the equipment, safety procedures, and emergency response.

Handover: The final stage of commissioning is the handover to operations. This involves transferring responsibility for the refinery from the construction team to the operations team, and ensuring that all necessary documentation, procedures, and training have been completed.

In conclusion, construction and commissioning are critical stages in the development of a refinery. The construction phase requires careful project management, health and safety measures, and quality control. The commissioning phase involves testing and adjusting the equipment to ensure that it is operating correctly and safely, and providing staff training and handover to operations.

SITE PREPARATION AND GRADING

Site preparation and grading are crucial aspects of building a refinery. Proper site preparation is essential for a safe and efficient construction process, while grading ensures that the site is level and allows for efficient drainage.

Site Preparation:

The first step in site preparation is to clear the land of any vegetation, debris, or other obstructions. This may involve the use of heavy equipment such as bulldozers, excavators, or backhoes. Once the land is cleared, the next step is to compact the soil to provide a stable foundation for the construction.

Before any construction activities can begin, the site must be properly fenced and secured to prevent unauthorized access. The site should also have access roads and parking areas for construction vehicles and personnel.

Grading:

Grading is the process of leveling the site and creating a slope to ensure proper drainage. Proper grading is essential to prevent standing water, erosion, and other drainage issues that can compromise the stability of the refinery.

The grading process typically involves the use of heavy equipment such as bulldozers, scrapers, and graders. The soil is excavated, leveled, and compacted to create the required slope and ensure proper drainage.

In addition to grading, the site may also require the installation of drainage systems, such as culverts or ditches, to manage stormwater runoff.

Overall, proper site preparation and grading are essential for the safe and efficient construction of a refinery. By ensuring a stable foundation and efficient drainage, the construction process can proceed smoothly, minimizing the risk of delays, accidents, and environmental damage.

Construction of Foundations, Storage Tanks, and Pipelines

Construction of foundations, storage tanks, and pipelines are some of the critical aspects of building a refinery. In this section, we will discuss each of these in detail.

Foundations:

Foundations are critical for supporting heavy equipment and structures such as distillation towers, compressors, and pumps. The construction of foundations typically involves the following steps:

Excavation: The first step is to excavate the site to the required depth and dimensions for the foundation.

Formwork: Formwork is used to create a mold for the concrete foundation. The formwork is typically made of wood, steel, or aluminum and is secured in place using steel reinforcing bars.

Pouring concrete: Once the formwork is in place, concrete is poured into the mold and allowed to cure.

Reinforcement: Steel reinforcement bars, or rebar, are embedded in the concrete to provide additional strength and durability.

Storage Tanks: Storage tanks are used to store crude oil and other products such as gasoline, diesel, and jet fuel. The construction of storage tanks typically involves the following steps:

Site preparation: The site is prepared, and the foundation is constructed.

Fabrication: The tank is fabricated offsite, typically in sections, and transported to the site for assembly.

Assembly: The tank sections are assembled on site, and the welding is completed to create a watertight seal.

Testing: The tank is tested for leaks and other defects before it is put into service.

Pipelines: Pipelines are used to transport crude oil, refined products, and other materials within the refinery and to and from other facilities. The construction of pipelines typically involves the following steps:

Routing: The route of the pipeline is determined, taking into account factors such as terrain, environmental concerns, and safety.

Excavation: Trenches are excavated for the pipeline, and any necessary culverts or other structures are installed.

Pipe installation: The pipe is installed in the trench, and any necessary fittings and valves are attached.

Testing: The pipeline is tested for leaks, strength, and durability before it is put into service.

Overall, the construction of foundations, storage tanks, and pipelines is critical for the safe and efficient operation of a refinery. By following proper construction practices, including appropriate site preparation, quality control, and testing, the refinery can be constructed to meet the required standards and provide reliable and safe operation.

INSTALLATION OF PROCESS EQUIPMENT AND INSTRUMENTATION

The installation of process equipment and instrumentation is a critical aspect of building a refinery. In this section, we will discuss the steps involved in the installation of process equipment and instrumentation.

Equipment Installation:

The installation of process equipment such as distillation towers, reactors, compressors, and pumps involves the following steps:

Positioning: The equipment is positioned in its designated location.

Alignment: The equipment is aligned to ensure that it is level and properly connected to adjacent equipment and piping.

Mounting: The equipment is mounted on its foundation or support structure.

Connection: The equipment is connected to adjacent piping and instrumentation, including valves, pumps, and other devices.

Testing: The equipment is tested to ensure that it is operating correctly and is leak-free.

Instrumentation Installation: Instrumentation plays a critical role in monitoring and controlling the various processes within the refinery. The installation of instrumentation involves the following steps:

Selection: The appropriate instrumentation is selected based on the process requirements.

Mounting: The instrumentation is mounted on its designated location, such as a pipeline, tank, or vessel.

Wiring: The wiring is connected to the control panel or distributed control system.

Calibration: The instrumentation is calibrated to ensure accurate measurements and control.

Testing: The instrumentation is tested to ensure that it is operating correctly and is providing accurate measurements.

Overall, the installation of process equipment and instrumentation requires careful planning, coordination, and execution to ensure that the refinery is built to meet the required standards and is capable of providing reliable and safe operation. By following proper installation practices, including appropriate alignment, connection, testing, and calibration, the refinery can be built to operate efficiently and meet the required specifications.

ELECTRICAL AND CONTROL SYSTEMS

Electrical and control systems are critical components of a refinery, and their design and installation require careful planning and execution. In this section, we will discuss the key aspects of electrical and control systems in a refinery.

ELECTRICAL SYSTEMS

The electrical system in a refinery includes power distribution, lighting, grounding, and other related components. The installation of electrical systems involves the following steps:

Electrical design: The electrical design is prepared based on the process requirements and regulatory requirements.

Electrical distribution: The power supply is distributed throughout the refinery using transformers, switchgear, and distribution panels.

Lighting: Lighting is installed throughout the refinery to provide adequate visibility for personnel and equipment.

Grounding: The electrical system is grounded to ensure safe operation and to protect equipment and personnel from electrical hazards.

Testing: The electrical system is tested to ensure that it is operating correctly and safely.

CONTROL SYSTEMS

Control systems are used to monitor and control the various processes within the refinery, including temperature, pressure, flow, and other critical parameters. The installation of control systems involves the following steps:

Control system design: The control system design is prepared based on the process requirements and regulatory requirements.

Instrumentation: The appropriate instrumentation is installed to measure the various process parameters.

Control panels: The control panels are installed to provide the necessary control and monitoring functions.

Wiring: The wiring is connected to the control panels and distributed to the various equipment and instrumentation.

Testing: The control system is tested to ensure that it is operating correctly and is providing accurate measurements and control.

Overall, the installation of electrical and control systems in a refinery requires careful planning, design, installation, and testing to ensure that the refinery is built to meet the required standards and is capable of providing reliable and safe operation. By following proper installation practices, including appropriate design, distribution, grounding, and testing, the refinery can be built to operate efficiently and meet the required specifications.

TESTING AND COMMISSIONING OF THE REFINERY

Testing and commissioning of a refinery is a critical process that involves the verification and validation of all the components and systems to ensure that they are operating correctly and safely. In this section, we will discuss the key steps involved in the testing and commissioning of a refinery.

PRE-COMMISSIONING ACTIVITIES

Pre-commissioning activities include the following steps:

Cleaning: All equipment, piping, and vessels are thoroughly cleaned to remove any debris or contaminants.

Inspection: All components and systems are inspected to ensure that they are properly installed and ready for commissioning.

Testing: Various tests are performed to verify the integrity and reliability of the equipment and systems.

Preparation of procedures: Procedures are developed to guide the commissioning process.

COMMISSIONING ACTIVITIES

Commissioning activities include the following steps:

Equipment and system testing: Each equipment and system is tested to verify that it is operating correctly and meets the required specifications.

Performance testing: A series of tests are performed to verify that the refinery is operating as intended and that it meets the performance requirements.

Functional testing: Each system and component is tested to verify that it is operating correctly and that it is integrated properly with other systems and components.

Operational testing: The refinery is operated under normal and abnormal conditions to verify that it can handle various process scenarios.

FINAL ACTIVITIES

Final activities include the following steps:

Documentation: All testing and commissioning activities are documented to ensure that they can be audited and verified in the future.

Handover: The refinery is handed over to the operations team.

Training: The operations team is trained on the operation and maintenance of the refinery.

Post-commissioning support: The commissioning team provides support to the operations team during the initial period of operation.

Overall, the testing and commissioning of a refinery require careful planning, execution, and documentation to ensure that the refinery is operating correctly and safely. By following proper commissioning practices, including appropriate testing, verification, and documentation, the refinery can be commissioned to meet the required standards and specifications.

Chapter 4

OPERATION AND MAINTENANCE

Once the refinery has been constructed and commissioned, it enters into the operational phase, which involves the day-to-day running of the plant. In this chapter, we will discuss the key aspects of operation and maintenance of a refinery.

OPERATION

The operation of a refinery involves the following key aspects:

Process control: The process parameters such as temperature, pressure, flow, and level are monitored and controlled to ensure that the refinery is operating within the specified parameters.

Production planning: The production plan is prepared based on the market demand and the available resources.

Safety and environmental management: The refinery should be operated safely to protect personnel and equipment, and also to minimize the impact on the environment.

Quality control: The product quality is monitored and controlled to ensure that it meets the required specifications.

Maintenance

The maintenance of a refinery involves the following key aspects:

Preventive maintenance: The equipment and systems are maintained on a regular basis to prevent any unexpected breakdowns and to ensure their longevity.

Predictive maintenance: The equipment and systems are monitored using various tools to predict any potential failures, and appropriate actions are taken to prevent them.

Corrective maintenance: In case of any breakdowns or failures, the equipment and systems are repaired or replaced as necessary.

Shutdown maintenance: During planned shutdowns, major maintenance activities such as overhauls or replacements are carried out.

TRAINING

The personnel involved in the operation and maintenance of a refinery should be well trained and skilled. The training should cover the following aspects:

Safety and environmental management: The personnel should be trained on the safety and environmental management systems of the refinery.

Process control: The personnel should be trained on the process control systems and should be familiar with the various process parameters.

Maintenance: The maintenance personnel should be trained on the various maintenance procedures and should have the necessary skills and knowledge to carry out their tasks.

Overall, the operation and maintenance of a refinery require careful planning, execution, and documentation to ensure that the refinery is operating safely and efficiently. By following proper operation and maintenance practices, including appropriate process control, maintenance, and training, the refinery can be operated and maintained to meet the required standards and specifications.

START-UP PROCEDURES AND INITIAL OPERATIONS

Before a refinery can begin operations, it must go through a start-up phase, which involves a series of steps to ensure that the equipment and systems are operating properly and that the product quality meets the required specifications. Here are the general start-up procedures for a refinery:

Safety checks:

Before starting any equipment or systems, safety checks must be performed to ensure that all safety devices are in place and functioning properly. This includes checking the fire and gas detection systems, emergency shutdown systems, and other safety devices.

Testing and commissioning:

The equipment and systems must be tested and commissioned to ensure that they are operating properly. This includes checking the instrumentation and control systems, verifying that the equipment is properly connected and aligned, and running the equipment at low speeds to check for any abnormalities.

Pre-commissioning activities:

Before introducing feedstock to the refinery, pre-commissioning activities must be completed. This includes flushing and cleaning the piping systems, filling the process vessels with water, and performing leak tests.

Feedstock introduction:

Once the pre-commissioning activities have been completed, feedstock can be introduced into the refinery. The feedstock is typically introduced into the atmospheric distillation unit (ADU), which separates the crude oil into various fractions.

Product quality control:

During the start-up phase, product quality is closely monitored to ensure that it meets the required specifications. This includes checking the product for impurities, ensuring that the product meets the required density and viscosity specifications, and verifying that the product meets other quality requirements.

Optimization:

As the refinery begins to operate, the processes are optimized to ensure maximum efficiency and product yield. This includes adjusting the process parameters such as temperature, pressure, and flow rates to achieve the desired product yield.

Overall, the start-up phase is a critical stage in the operation of a refinery. Proper planning and execution of start-up procedures can help ensure that the refinery operates safely and efficiently, and that the product quality meets the required specifications.

OPERATING THE REFINERY EFFICIENTLY AND SAFELY

Operating a refinery efficiently and safely requires a comprehensive approach that involves a combination of processes, procedures, and systems. Here are some of the key considerations for operating a refinery efficiently and safely:

Process control:

Process control systems are used to monitor and control the various processes in the refinery. These systems use sensors, control valves, and other instrumentation to measure and control variables such as temperature, pressure, and flow rate. By maintaining tight control over these variables, the refinery can operate more efficiently and reduce the risk of accidents and product quality issues.

Maintenance:

Regular maintenance is essential for keeping the refinery running smoothly and preventing downtime due to equipment failure. This includes routine inspections, lubrication, and replacement of worn parts. Maintenance schedules should be developed based on the specific needs of the equipment and processes in the refinery.

Training and education:

Proper training and education of personnel is critical for operating a refinery safely and efficiently. This includes training on the specific equipment and processes used in the refinery, as well as safety procedures and emergency response protocols. Personnel should also be trained on how to respond to abnormal operating conditions and how to prevent and mitigate potential hazards.

Safety systems:

Safety systems such as fire and gas detection, emergency shutdown, and flare systems are essential for protecting personnel and the environment in the event of an accident. These systems should be regularly tested and maintained to ensure that they are functioning properly.

Environmental compliance:

Refineries are subject to a range of environmental regulations and requirements, including air emissions, water discharge, and waste management. Compliance with these regulations is critical for protecting the environment and avoiding fines and penalties.

Continuous improvement:

Continuous improvement programs are used to identify opportunities for improving efficiency, reducing costs, and enhancing safety. These programs may include regular audits, data analysis, and feedback from personnel.

Overall, operating a refinery efficiently and safely requires a holistic approach that encompasses all aspects of the operation. By implementing best practices and continuously monitoring and improving operations, refineries can operate safely, reliably, and efficiently.

MONITORING AND CONTROLLING REFINERY PROCESSES

Monitoring and controlling refinery processes is critical to ensuring that the refinery operates safely and efficiently. Here are some of the key ways that refinery processes are monitored and controlled:

Process instrumentation: Process instrumentation, such as sensors and gauges, are used to measure key variables such as temperature, pressure, and flow rate. This data is then used to control the various processes in the refinery. For example, if the temperature of a reactor vessel gets too high, the instrumentation can send a signal to a control valve to reduce the flow of reactants.

Distributed control systems (DCS): DCS is a computerized system used to control and monitor the various processes in the refinery. DCS systems are used to automate processes, improve efficiency, and reduce the risk of human error. DCS systems use sensors and other instrumentation to collect data, which is then processed and used to control the various processes in the refinery.

Advanced process control (APC): APC uses mathematical models and algorithms to optimize refinery processes in real-time. APC systems can improve efficiency and reduce costs by optimizing process parameters and identifying opportunities for process improvements. APC systems are often used in conjunction with DCS systems to provide more advanced control and optimization capabilities.

Safety systems: Refineries use a range of safety systems to protect personnel and equipment in the event of an accident. These systems include fire and gas detection systems, emergency shutdown systems, and flare systems. These systems are often integrated into the DCS system to provide real-time monitoring and control of safety systems.

Operator training and response: Operators play a critical role in monitoring and controlling refinery processes. They are responsible for monitoring process variables and responding to abnormal conditions. Proper operator training and response protocols are critical for ensuring that the refinery operates safely and efficiently.

Overall, monitoring and controlling refinery processes is a complex and critical process. Refineries use a combination of instrumentation, computerized systems, and human operators to ensure that the refinery operates safely and efficiently.

TROUBLESHOOTING AND PROBLEM-SOLVING

Despite the best efforts to maintain and optimize refinery processes, problems can still occur. Troubleshooting and problem-solving are essential skills for refinery personnel to quickly diagnose and resolve issues that arise. Here are some steps for troubleshooting and problem-solving in a refinery:

Identify the problem:

The first step in troubleshooting is to identify the problem. This can involve gathering information from instrumentation, reviewing operating procedures, and speaking with operators or other personnel.

Define the problem:

Once the problem has been identified, it is important to define the problem clearly. This involves defining the symptoms, the location of the problem, and any other relevant details.

Develop hypotheses:

After the problem has been defined, hypotheses can be developed to explain the problem. These hypotheses should be based on an understanding of the refinery processes and any other relevant information.

Test hypotheses:

Once hypotheses have been developed, they should be tested to see if they explain the problem. This can involve checking instrumentation, reviewing operating procedures, and making adjustments to equipment or processes.

Implement solutions:

After the problem has been diagnosed, solutions can be implemented to resolve the issue. This can involve making adjustments to equipment or processes, modifying operating procedures, or making repairs.

Monitor and verify:

After the solution has been implemented, it is important to monitor the process to ensure that the problem has been resolved. This can involve checking instrumentation, reviewing operating procedures, and verifying that the problem has been resolved.

Document:

It is important to document the troubleshooting and problem-solving process. This can help to identify similar problems in the future and develop procedures to prevent them from occurring.

Overall, troubleshooting and problem-solving are critical skills for refinery personnel to quickly diagnose and resolve issues that arise. By following a structured approach, problems can be resolved quickly and efficiently, minimizing the impact on the refinery processes.

PREVENTIVE AND PREDICTIVE MAINTENANCE

Preventive maintenance and predictive maintenance are two important strategies for maintaining refinery equipment and reducing downtime. Here's a brief overview of each:

Preventive maintenance:

Preventive maintenance involves regularly scheduled maintenance tasks designed to prevent equipment failure. This includes activities like lubrication, inspection, and replacement of parts before they reach the end of their useful life. The goal of preventive maintenance is to keep equipment running smoothly and avoid unplanned downtime.

Some examples of preventive maintenance tasks for a refinery might include:

Regularly inspecting and cleaning equipment to prevent corrosion or buildup

Lubricating machinery and replacing worn parts

Replacing filters and other consumable items on a regular schedule

Calibrating instrumentation to ensure accurate readings.

Predictive maintenance

Predictive maintenance involves using data and analysis to predict when equipment is likely to fail, so that maintenance can be scheduled before the failure occurs. This can involve monitoring equipment performance and analyzing data to identify patterns or trends that indicate impending failure. Some examples of predictive maintenance tasks for a refinery might include:

Using vibration analysis to identify worn or damaged bearings

Monitoring process parameters to detect changes that could indicate equipment failure

Using infrared imaging to identify hot spots or other abnormalities in equipment

By combining preventive and predictive maintenance strategies, refineries can reduce downtime and improve equipment reliability. Preventive maintenance helps to keep equipment running smoothly, while predictive maintenance helps to identify potential problems before they cause unplanned downtime.

Emergency response procedures

Emergency response procedures are critical for ensuring the safety of refinery personnel and minimizing damage in the event of an emergency. Here are some key elements of an effective emergency response plan:

Emergency response team:

The emergency response team should include personnel with the necessary training and expertise to respond to different types of emergencies. This may include fire fighters, medical personnel, and other specialists.

Emergency procedures:

Emergency procedures should be clearly defined and communicated to all refinery personnel. This includes procedures for responding to fires, spills, releases, and other emergencies.

Emergency equipment:

The refinery should be equipped with the necessary emergency equipment, including fire suppression systems, spill response equipment, and personal protective equipment.

Training and drills:

All personnel should receive regular training on emergency response procedures and participate in emergency drills to ensure that they are familiar with the procedures and can respond effectively in the event of an emergency.

Communication:

Effective communication is essential during an emergency. The emergency response team should have a communication plan in place to ensure that they can communicate with each other and with other personnel as needed.

Evacuation:

Evacuation procedures should be defined and communicated to all personnel. This includes procedures for evacuating the refinery in the event of an emergency, as well as procedures for accounting for personnel after an evacuation.

Post-emergency procedures:

After an emergency, it is important to conduct an investigation to determine the cause of the emergency and identify any necessary corrective actions. The results of the investigation should be communicated to all personnel and incorporated into the emergency response plan as needed.

By following these key elements of an effective emergency response plan, refineries can help to ensure the safety of personnel and minimize the impact of emergencies.

Chapter 5

PRODUCT QUALITY AND DISTRIBUTION

P roduct quality and distribution are critical aspects of refinery operation. Here are some key considerations:

Product quality:

Refineries must ensure that the products they produce meet the required quality standards. This includes meeting regulatory requirements for emissions, as well as meeting specifications for product quality such as octane rating, viscosity, and sulfur content. Refineries may use a variety of techniques to control product quality, including blending, catalysts, and process control systems.

Storage and transportation:

Once products have been produced, they must be stored and transported to customers. Refineries may have on-site storage tanks for finished products, as well as pipelines, trucks, and railcars for transportation. Refineries must ensure that their storage and transportation systems are properly maintained and operated to ensure product quality and safety.

Supply chain management:

Refineries must manage their supply chain to ensure that they have the necessary raw materials and components to produce their products. This includes managing the procurement of crude oil and other feedstocks, as well as managing relationships with suppliers of equipment and other materials.

Marketing and sales:

Refineries must have effective marketing and sales strategies to sell their products. This may involve selling to wholesale customers such as gasoline retailers and industrial customers, as well as selling to end users such as consumers. Refineries must also manage pricing and distribution to ensure that they remain competitive in the market.

Regulatory compliance:

Refineries must comply with a range of regulatory requirements related to product quality, emissions, safety, and other factors. This includes complying with federal, state, and local regulations, as well as industry standards and best practices. Refineries must also maintain accurate records and submit reports to regulatory agencies as required.

By paying careful attention to product quality and distribution, refineries can ensure that they remain competitive and compliant while delivering high-quality products to their customers.

QUALITY CONTROL AND ASSURANCE

Quality control and assurance are critical aspects of refinery operation. Refineries must ensure that the products they produce meet the required quality standards, including regulatory requirements for emissions, as well as meeting specifications for product quality such as octane rating, viscosity, and sulfur content.

Here are some key considerations for quality control and assurance in refinery operations:

Testing and analysis:

Refineries use a range of testing and analysis techniques to monitor product quality throughout the refining process. This includes analyzing crude oil and other feedstocks for impurities, as well as testing finished products for properties such as octane rating, viscosity, and sulfur content.

Process control systems:

Refineries use process control systems to monitor and control the refining process. These systems use sensors and other monitoring equipment to measure key parameters such as temperature, pressure, and flow rate, and then use algorithms to adjust process parameters as needed to ensure that the finished product meets quality specifications.

Quality management systems:

Refineries use quality management systems to ensure that quality standards are consistently met throughout the organization. This may include implementing standardized operating procedures, providing training to employees, and conducting regular audits to ensure that processes are being followed correctly.

Continuous improvement:

Refineries should have a process in place for continuous improvement, including analyzing data and identifying opportunities to improve product quality and operational efficiency. This may involve implementing new technologies, improving process control systems, or making other changes to the refining process.

By implementing robust quality control and assurance processes, refineries can ensure that they consistently produce high-quality products that meet regulatory requirements and customer specifications. This can help to improve operational efficiency, reduce costs, and enhance customer satisfaction.

Testing and inspection of products

Testing and inspection of products is an important aspect of quality control and assurance in refinery operations. Refineries use a variety of methods to test and inspect their products to ensure that they meet the required quality standards and specifications.

Here are some of the key methods used for testing and inspection of products in refineries:

Laboratory testing:

Refineries have on-site laboratories where they conduct tests on samples of their products. These tests can include physical and chemical analysis, as well as tests for contaminants and impurities.

On-line monitoring:

Refineries use on-line monitoring systems to measure key parameters in real-time as products are being produced. This helps to ensure that the refining process is operating within the desired parameters and that the final product meets quality specifications.

Inspection:

Refineries conduct regular inspections of their equipment and facilities to ensure that they are operating properly and that there are no leaks or other issues that could affect product quality. This can include visual inspections, as well as more detailed inspections using specialized equipment.

Certification:

Refineries may seek certification from third-party organizations to demonstrate that their products meet certain quality standards. This can be important for marketing and sales purposes, as it helps to build customer confidence in the quality of the products.

By using these methods for testing and inspection, refineries can ensure that their products meet the required quality standards and specifications. This helps to ensure customer satisfaction and can also help to prevent costly product recalls and other issues that could impact the reputation of the refinery.

STORAGE AND HANDLING OF FINISHED PRODUCTS

Storage and handling of finished products is a critical aspect of refinery operations. Proper storage and handling help to ensure that finished products maintain their quality and integrity until they are shipped to customers.

Here are some key considerations for storage and handling of finished products in a refinery:

Storage tanks:

Finished products are typically stored in large tanks within the refinery. These tanks must be designed to meet specific requirements for the type of product being stored, such as temperature, pressure, and corrosion resistance.

Transfer lines:

Finished products are typically transferred from the storage tanks to shipping containers using pipelines or other transfer lines. These transfer lines must be designed and maintained to prevent leaks or spills that could impact the quality of the product.

Loading and unloading:

Finished products are typically loaded onto trucks, railcars, or ships for transport to customers. Refineries must have proper loading and unloading facilities to ensure that products are handled safely and efficiently.

Quality control:

Refineries must conduct quality control checks on finished products before they are shipped to customers. This can include laboratory testing to ensure that the product meets specifications for purity, viscosity, and other parameters.

Environmental considerations:

Refineries must also consider environmental factors when storing and handling finished products. This can include ensuring that storage tanks and transfer lines are designed to prevent leaks or spills that could impact the environment, as well as managing the disposal of any waste or byproducts generated during the refining process.

By following these best practices for storage and handling of finished products, refineries can ensure that their products maintain their quality and integrity until they are delivered to customers. This helps to ensure customer satisfaction and can also help to prevent costly product recalls or other issues that could impact the reputation of the refinery.

Transportation and distribution of products

Transportation and distribution of products are crucial components of the refinery operations as they involve the shipment of finished products from the refinery to customers, which can be located domestically or internationally. There are several modes of transportation that can be used, including pipelines, trucks, rail, and marine vessels.

Here are some key considerations for transportation and distribution of products from a refinery:

Mode of transportation:

Each mode of transportation has its advantages and disadvantages. Pipelines are typically the most cost-effective mode of transportation for large volumes of product over long distances. Trucks and rail are suitable for shorter distances and can provide greater flexibility in terms of routing. Marine vessels are suitable for transporting large volumes of product over long distances but require extensive infrastructure at the ports.

Logistics and supply chain management:

Transportation and distribution require careful planning and management to ensure that products are delivered to customers in a timely and cost-effective manner. This can involve coordinating with suppliers, customers, and transportation providers to ensure that products are available when and where they are needed.

Regulatory compliance:

Transportation and distribution are subject to a range of regulations and standards that must be followed to ensure the safety of the product and the public. This can include regulations related to product labeling, packaging, and transport.

Security:

Transportation and distribution of products are vulnerable to theft, tampering, and other security threats. Refineries must have proper security measures in place to ensure the integrity of the product throughout the transportation and distribution process.

Environmental considerations:

Transportation and distribution of products can also have environmental impacts, such as air pollution and greenhouse gas emissions. Refineries must consider these impacts when selecting transportation modes and work to minimize them where possible.

By carefully managing the transportation and distribution of products, refineries can ensure that their products are delivered to customers safely, efficiently, and cost-effectively. This helps to ensure customer satisfaction and can also help to build a positive reputation for the refinery.

COMPLIANCE WITH REGULATORY REQUIREMENTS

Compliance with regulatory requirements is critical for the safe and effective operation of a refinery. Refineries must comply with a range of local, state, federal, and international regulations related to health, safety, and environmental protection. These regulations are designed to protect workers, the public, and the environment from potential hazards associated with refinery operations.

Here are some key areas where refineries must comply with regulatory requirements:

Permitting and reporting:

Refineries must obtain the necessary permits from regulatory agencies before they can begin construction and operation. These permits typically require detailed information about the refinery's operations and may include limits on emissions, discharge, and waste management. Refineries must also submit regular reports to regulatory agencies to demonstrate compliance with permit conditions.

Air emissions:

Refineries are significant sources of air emissions, including volatile organic compounds (VOCs), particulate matter, sulfur dioxide (SO2), and nitrogen oxides (NOx). Refineries must comply with regulations related to air emissions, including limits on emissions, monitoring requirements, and reporting requirements.

Water and wastewater management:

Refineries generate large volumes of wastewater, which can contain pollutants such as oil, grease, metals, and chemicals. Refineries must comply with regulations related to the discharge of wastewater, including limits on the types and quantities of pollutants that can be discharged. Refineries must also have systems in place to treat and manage wastewater before it is discharged.

Hazardous waste management:

Refineries generate hazardous waste, including spent catalysts, sludges, and contaminated materials. Refineries must comply with regulations related to the storage, handling, treatment, and disposal of hazardous waste.

Occupational health and safety:

Refineries must comply with regulations related to occupational health and safety, including requirements for personal protective equipment, hazard communication, and emergency response.

Transportation and distribution:

Refineries must comply with regulations related to the transportation and distribution of products, including regulations related to labeling, packaging, and transport.

By complying with regulatory requirements, refineries can ensure that they are operating safely and in an environmentally responsible manner. This helps to protect the health and safety of workers, the public, and the environment and can also help to maintain the refinery's reputation and social license to operate.

Chapter 6

ECONOMICS AND FINANCE

B uilding and running a refinery is a significant investment that requires careful consideration of economic and financial factors. In this chapter, we will explore some of the key economic and financial considerations associated with refineries.

Capital costs:

The capital costs associated with building a refinery can be significant. These costs include the cost of land, construction materials, equipment, and labor. To minimize capital costs, refineries may opt to purchase used equipment or modular units.

Operating costs:

Operating costs include the cost of raw materials, labor, energy, maintenance, and other expenses associated with running the refinery. To minimize operating costs, refineries may invest in energy-efficient technologies or employ cost-saving measures, such as process optimization or waste reduction.

Profitability:

Profitability is a critical consideration when building and running a refinery. Refineries generate revenue by selling refined products, such as gasoline, diesel, and jet fuel. The profitability of a refinery is dependent on a range of factors, including the price of crude oil, the demand for refined products, and the refinery's operating efficiency.

Financing:

Financing the construction of a refinery requires significant capital investment, and many refineries are financed through a combination of debt and equity. Financing options include bank loans, bonds, and public offerings. It is important to carefully consider the terms and conditions of financing options to ensure that they are financially viable over the long term.

Risk management:

Building and running a refinery involves a range of risks, including market risk, operational risk, and environmental risk. Risk management strategies may include insurance policies, risk mitigation measures, and contingency planning.

Regulatory compliance:

Compliance with regulatory requirements is essential for the safe and effective operation of a refinery. Regulatory compliance can have a significant impact on the economics and finances of a refinery. Refineries must allocate resources to comply with regulatory requirements, which can increase operating costs.

Overall, building and running a refinery requires careful consideration of economic and financial factors. By carefully assessing these factors, refineries can minimize costs, optimize profitability, and ensure long-term financial viability.

COST ESTIMATION AND PROJECT BUDGETING

Cost estimation and project budgeting are critical components of building and running a refinery. A detailed cost estimate and budget are necessary to ensure that the project is financially viable and that the capital investment can be recouped over the life of the refinery. In this section, we will explore the process of cost estimation and project budgeting for a refinery.

Cost estimation:

The first step in cost estimation is to identify the major cost components of the project. This includes the cost of land, construction materials, equipment, labor, engineering, and other indirect costs such as permits and licenses. A detailed cost estimate is then prepared for each cost component based on the scope of work and other project-specific parameters. It is important to involve all relevant stakeholders, including engineers, contractors, and vendors, in the cost estimation process to ensure that all cost factors are identified and included in the estimate.

Project budgeting:

Once the cost estimate is complete, the project budget can be developed. The project budget is a comprehensive financial plan that outlines the costs associated with the project and the sources of funding. The budget should include a contingency fund to account for unexpected costs or changes in the scope of work.

Cost control:

Cost control is essential to ensure that the project stays within budget. A project manager should be appointed to oversee the project and manage costs. The project manager should be responsible for tracking actual costs against the budget, identifying cost overruns, and implementing corrective measures to bring the project back on track. It is important to establish a system for regular reporting and monitoring of costs to ensure that the project stays on budget.

Life-cycle cost analysis:

Life-cycle cost analysis is a technique used to evaluate the costs associated with a project over its entire life cycle. This includes the costs associated with construction, operation, maintenance, and decommissioning. Life-cycle cost analysis can help to identify cost-saving measures that can be implemented during the design and construction phases of the project to minimize costs over the life of the refinery.

In conclusion, cost estimation and project budgeting are critical components of building and running a refinery. By carefully estimating costs, developing a comprehensive project budget, implementing cost control measures, and conducting life-cycle cost analysis, refineries can ensure that the project is financially viable and that the capital investment can be recouped over the life of the refinery.

SOURCES OF FUNDING AND FINANCING OPTIONS

Sources of funding and financing options are critical considerations when building and running a refinery. The capital cost of a refinery can be significant, and there are several options available to fund the project.

Debt financing:

Debt financing involves borrowing money from banks or other financial institutions to finance the project. The borrower agrees to repay the loan with interest over a specified period. Debt financing can be attractive because the interest on the loan is tax-deductible and may be lower than the cost of equity financing. However, debt financing also comes with the risk of default, which can result in severe financial consequences.

Equity financing:

Equity financing involves raising capital by selling ownership shares in the company. Investors purchase shares in the company in exchange for a stake in the ownership and a share of the profits. Equity financing can be attractive because it does not require repayment, and investors share the risk of the project. However, equity financing can be costly, and the ownership structure of the company may be diluted if too many shares are issued.

Government financing:

Governments may offer financing options for refineries to promote economic development and energy security. This financing can take the form of grants, loans, or tax incentives. Government financing can be attractive because it may have lower interest rates, longer repayment periods, or favorable tax treatment. However, government financing may come with additional regulatory requirements or political risks.

Joint ventures:

Joint ventures involve two or more companies pooling resources to build and operate a refinery. Each partner contributes capital, expertise, or other resources to the project and shares in the ownership and profits. Joint ventures can be attractive because they allow for shared risk and the ability to leverage complementary skills and resources. However, joint ventures can also be complex and require significant negotiation and coordination.

In conclusion, funding and financing options are critical considerations when building and running a refinery. Debt financing, equity financing, government financing, and joint ventures are all viable options, and the choice of financing will depend on the specific circumstances of the project. It is essential to work with a team of financial experts to evaluate the options and make an informed decision that ensures the financial viability of the project.

ECONOMIC ANALYSIS AND PROFITABILITY ASSESSMENT

Economic analysis and profitability assessment are critical aspects of building and running a refinery. It is essential to evaluate the financial viability of the project to ensure that it will generate sufficient profits to cover the capital and operating costs and provide a return on investment.

Capital cost estimation:

Capital cost estimation is the process of estimating the total cost of building the refinery. The capital cost includes the cost of land, construction, equipment, infrastructure, and other associated costs. It is essential to conduct a thorough cost estimation to determine the initial capital required to build the refinery accurately.

Operating cost estimation:

Operating cost estimation is the process of estimating the ongoing expenses required to operate and maintain the refinery. The operating cost includes expenses such as labor, utilities, raw materials, maintenance, and other associated costs. It is essential to conduct a thorough operating cost estimation to determine the ongoing expenses required to keep the refinery operational.

Profitability analysis:

Profitability analysis is the process of evaluating the potential profits of the refinery. It involves comparing the revenue generated by the refinery to the capital and operating costs. It is essential to evaluate the profitability of the refinery to ensure that it will generate sufficient profits to cover the expenses and provide a return on investment.

Sensitivity analysis:

Sensitivity analysis is the process of evaluating how changes in key variables will impact the profitability of the refinery. It is essential to conduct sensitivity analysis to identify potential risks and determine the robustness of the refinery's financial projections.

Risk analysis:

Risk analysis is the process of identifying potential risks associated with the refinery and evaluating the likelihood and impact of those risks. It is essential to conduct risk analysis to identify potential threats to the refinery's profitability and develop strategies to mitigate those risks.

In conclusion, economic analysis and profitability assessment are critical aspects of building and running a refinery. It is essential to conduct thorough capital and operating cost estimation, profitability analysis, sensitivity analysis, and risk analysis to ensure the financial viability of the project. Working with a team of financial experts can help ensure that the refinery is profitable and sustainable in the long run.

MARKET ANALYSIS AND PRICING STRATEGIES

Market analysis and pricing strategies are also essential aspects of building and running a refinery. Understanding the market demand and competition for the products produced by the refinery is critical to developing pricing strategies that will maximize profitability.

Market analysis:

Market analysis is the process of evaluating market demand and competition for the products produced by the refinery. It involves analyzing market trends, identifying potential customers, evaluating competition, and assessing the potential demand for the products produced by the refinery. A thorough market analysis can help identify potential opportunities and challenges for the refinery.

Product pricing:

Product pricing is the process of setting prices for the products produced by the refinery. It involves evaluating market demand, production costs, and competition to determine the optimal price for the products. A well-designed pricing strategy can help maximize profitability and ensure the competitiveness of the refinery in the market.

Sales and marketing:

Sales and marketing are critical aspects of running a refinery. It involves developing sales and marketing strategies to promote the products produced by the refinery and attract potential customers. Effective sales and marketing strategies can help increase the demand for the products and boost profitability.

Distribution channels:

Distribution channels are critical to delivering the products produced by the refinery to customers. It involves developing distribution channels that are efficient, cost-effective, and reliable. Effective distribution channels can help ensure that the products reach customers on time and in good condition, which can boost customer satisfaction and loyalty.

In conclusion, market analysis and pricing strategies are critical aspects of building and running a refinery. A thorough market analysis can help identify potential opportunities and challenges,

111

while effective pricing strategies, sales and marketing, and distribution channels can help maximize profitability and ensure the competitiveness of the refinery in the market. Working with a team of market experts can help ensure that the refinery's products are priced correctly and effectively marketed to potential customers.

RISK MANAGEMENT AND INSURANCE

Risk management and insurance are important aspects of building and running a refinery. The oil and gas industry is inherently risky, and refineries face a range of risks, including safety hazards, environmental risks, and financial risks. A comprehensive risk management plan can help identify and mitigate potential risks, while insurance coverage can provide financial protection in the event of unforeseen events.

Risk management:

Risk management is the process of identifying, assessing, and managing risks that may impact the refinery's operations, employees, and the environment. It involves implementing safety procedures, establishing emergency response plans, and conducting regular risk assessments. Effective risk management can help reduce the likelihood and impact of potential risks.

Insurance coverage:

Insurance coverage is essential for protecting the refinery from financial losses that may arise from accidents, equipment failure, or other unforeseen events. The types of insurance coverage required may vary depending on the size and type of the refinery, but typically include property insurance, liability insurance, and workers' compensation insurance. Working with an experienced insurance provider can help ensure that the refinery has appropriate coverage in place.

Regulatory compliance:

Regulatory compliance is another important aspect of risk management. Refineries must comply with a range of environmental, health, and safety regulations, and failure to comply can result in fines, penalties, and other legal consequences. Working with experienced regulatory consultants can help ensure that the refinery is in compliance with all applicable regulations and can help identify potential compliance issues before they become major problems.

In conclusion, risk management and insurance are important aspects of building and running a refinery. Effective risk management can help reduce the likelihood and impact of potential risks, while insurance coverage can provide financial protection in the event of unforeseen events. Regulatory compliance is also critical to ensuring the safety and environmental responsibility of the refinery. Working with experienced professionals can help ensure that the refinery is properly protected and in compliance with all applicable regulations.

Chapter 7

FUTURE TRENDS AND DEVELOPMENTS

As the oil and gas industry continues to evolve, refineries must adapt to changing market conditions, technological advancements, and environmental regulations. This chapter will explore some of the emerging trends and developments in the industry and their potential impact on refineries.

Renewable energy:

Renewable energy sources, such as wind and solar power, are becoming increasingly competitive with traditional fossil fuels. As governments around the world look to reduce their carbon footprint, refineries may need to consider diversifying into renewable energy production. This could involve the integration of renewable energy sources into the refinery's operations or the development of separate renewable energy facilities.

Digitalization:

The digitalization of the oil and gas industry is transforming how refineries operate. Advancements in data analytics, artificial intelligence, and automation are enabling refineries to optimize their processes and improve efficiency. Refineries that are able to embrace these new technologies may gain a competitive advantage in the market.

Carbon capture and storage:

Carbon capture and storage (CCS) technologies are being developed to capture and store carbon emissions from refineries and other industrial processes. This could help refineries reduce their carbon footprint and meet increasingly stringent environmental regulations. However, CCS technologies are still in the early stages of development, and their viability and cost-effectiveness have yet to be fully demonstrated.

Circular economy:

The circular economy is a model of production and consumption that aims to minimize waste and maximize the use of resources. Refineries may be able to contribute to the circular economy by recycling waste products and developing new products from recycled materials.

Energy efficiency:

Improving energy efficiency is a key priority for many refineries. This can involve optimizing processes to reduce energy consumption, as well as implementing energy-saving technologies and renewable energy sources. Improving energy efficiency can help reduce costs and improve the environmental sustainability of the refinery.

In conclusion, the oil and gas industry is undergoing significant changes, and refineries must adapt to remain competitive and meet changing regulatory requirements. The emerging trends and developments outlined in this chapter have the potential to significantly impact the industry and may present opportunities for refineries that are able to embrace them.

EMERGING TECHNOLOGIES IN THE REFINING INDUSTRY

The refining industry is constantly evolving, with new technologies emerging to improve efficiency, reduce costs, and minimize environmental impacts. Some of the emerging technologies in the refining industry include:

Advanced Process Control (APC): APC uses sophisticated software and analytics to optimize refinery processes in real-time. By adjusting process variables, such as temperature and pressure,

APC can improve product quality, reduce energy consumption, and increase throughput.

Renewable energy integration: With the growing demand for cleaner energy, many refineries are integrating renewable energy sources, such as solar and wind power, into their operations. This not only reduces greenhouse gas emissions but also provides a reliable source of electricity for the refinery.

Carbon capture and storage (CCS): CCS technology captures carbon dioxide emissions from the refinery and stores them underground, reducing greenhouse gas emissions. This technology is still in the early stages of development but has the potential to significantly reduce the environmental impact of refineries.

Process intensification: Process intensification involves reducing the size and complexity of equipment and processes to improve efficiency and reduce costs. This technology can be applied to a range of refinery processes, from distillation to catalytic cracking.

Digitalization and automation: Refineries are increasingly using digitalization and automation to improve efficiency and reduce costs. This includes the use of sensors and data analytics to monitor equipment and processes in real-time, as well as the use of robots and drones to perform maintenance and inspections.

Overall, these emerging technologies have the potential to revolutionize the refining industry, making it more efficient, cost-effective, and sustainable. Refineries that invest in these technologies will be well-positioned to succeed in a rapidly changing industry.

RENEWABLE ENERGY AND ITS IMPACT ON THE INDUSTRY

Renewable energy is having a growing impact on the refining industry. Traditionally, refineries have relied on fossil fuels, such as oil and natural gas, to power their operations. However, with the increasing demand for cleaner energy sources, many refineries are now incorporating renewable energy into their operations. There are several ways in which renewable energy is impacting the refining industry:

Cost savings: Renewable energy sources, such as solar and wind power, can provide a cheaper source of electricity for refineries. By using renewable energy, refineries can reduce their energy costs and improve their profitability.

Emissions reduction: Renewable energy sources emit significantly less greenhouse gases than traditional fossil fuels. By using renewable energy, refineries can reduce their carbon footprint and improve their environmental performance.

Energy security: By generating their own renewable energy, refineries can reduce their dependence on external energy sources, such as the grid. This can improve their energy security and reduce their exposure to price fluctuations in the energy market.

Regulatory compliance: Many countries and regions have introduced regulations aimed at reducing greenhouse gas emissions. By using renewable energy, refineries can comply with these regulations and avoid potential penalties.

Market demand: As consumers become more environmentally conscious, there is growing demand for products that are produced using renewable energy. By using renewable energy, refineries can meet this demand and improve their marketability.

Overall, renewable energy is having a significant impact on the refining industry, providing cost savings, emissions reductions, energy security, regulatory compliance, and improved marketability. As the cost of renewable energy continues to decline and the demand for cleaner energy sources continues to grow, it is likely that more and more refineries will incorporate renewable energy into their operations.

SUSTAINABILITY AND ENVIRONMENTAL CONSIDERATIONS

Sustainability and environmental considerations are becoming increasingly important in the refining industry. Refineries are significant energy users and can have a significant impact on the environment. As such, there are several key sustainability and environmental considerations that refineries need to take into account:

Energy efficiency: Refineries consume a significant amount of energy. By improving their energy efficiency, refineries can reduce their energy consumption and associated greenhouse gas emissions. This can be achieved through the use of energy-efficient equipment, process improvements, and the implementation of energy management systems.

Water usage: Refineries also consume a significant amount of water. By implementing water conservation measures, such as the use of recycled or reclaimed water, refineries can reduce their water consumption and associated environmental impact.

Air emissions: Refineries can emit a range of air pollutants, including sulfur dioxide, nitrogen oxides, and particulate matter. By implementing emission control technologies, such as catalytic converters and scrubbers, refineries can reduce their air emissions and associated environmental impact.

Waste management: Refineries generate a range of waste products, including hazardous and non-hazardous wastes. By implementing effective waste management practices, such as recycling, reusing, and disposing of waste in an environmentally responsible manner, refineries can reduce their environmental impact.

Sustainable sourcing: Refineries rely on a range of raw materials, such as crude oil and natural gas. By sourcing these materials from sustainable sources, such as renewable energy sources, refineries can reduce their environmental impact and support the development of a more sustainable energy industry.

Overall, sustainability and environmental considerations are critical for the long-term success of the refining industry. By prioritizing energy efficiency, water conservation, air emissions control, waste management, and sustainable sourcing, refineries can reduce their environmental impact, improve their sustainability, and enhance their social license to operate.

FUTURE CHALLENGES AND OPPORTUNITIES

As the world continues to evolve, the refining industry faces various challenges and opportunities. Some of the future challenges and opportunities include:

Increasing demand for cleaner energy: The world is becoming more environmentally conscious, and there is a growing demand for cleaner and more sustainable energy sources. This shift is likely to continue, and refineries must adapt to these changes by producing cleaner fuels and investing in renewable energy technologies.

Advancements in technology: Technology is rapidly evolving, and refineries must keep up with the latest advancements to remain competitive. Automation, artificial intelligence, and big data analytics are some of the technologies that refineries can use to optimize their operations and improve their bottom line.

Economic and geopolitical shifts: Economic and geopolitical changes can have a significant impact on the refining industry. Fluctuations in oil prices, changes in government policies, and geopolitical tensions can all affect the industry's profitability.

Infrastructure challenges: Infrastructure challenges, such as aging pipelines and storage facilities, can limit a refinery's capacity to transport and store crude oil and finished products. Refineries must invest in infrastructure upgrades to meet the growing demand for their products.

Skilled workforce shortage: The refining industry relies on a skilled workforce, and there is a shortage of qualified personnel in many parts of the world. Refineries must invest in training programs to develop their employees' skills and attract new talent to the industry.

Circular economy: The circular economy model aims to reduce waste and promote sustainability by reusing and recycling materials. Refineries can play a role in the circular economy by using waste materials as feedstocks for their processes or producing products that can be recycled or reused.

Carbon capture and storage: Carbon capture and storage (CCS) is a technology that captures carbon dioxide emissions from industrial processes and stores them underground. Refineries can use CCS to reduce their carbon footprint and comply with environmental regulations.

Overall, the refining industry must remain flexible and adaptable to meet the challenges and opportunities of the future. By investing in new technologies, promoting sustainability, and developing their workforce, refineries can position themselves for long-term success.

Chapter 8

CONCLUSION

In conclusion, building and running a refinery is a complex and challenging undertaking that requires careful planning, design, construction, operation, and maintenance. The benefits of owning and operating a refinery are significant, including increased control over the supply chain, improved profitability, and the ability to meet customer demand for high-quality products.

This book has covered the essential elements of building and running a refinery, including planning and design, construction and commissioning, operation and maintenance, product quality and distribution, economics and finance, and future trends and developments. By following the guidelines and best practices outlined in this book, refinery owners and operators can achieve long-term success and sustainability in this dynamic and ever-changing industry.

While the refining industry faces many challenges and uncertainties, it also offers exciting opportunities for innovation, growth, and environmental stewardship. As new technologies and renewable energy sources continue to emerge, the refining industry must adapt and evolve to meet the changing needs of society. With the right approach and mindset, building and running a refinery can be a rewarding and fulfilling experience for those who are committed to excellence, safety, and sustainability.

SUMMARY OF KEY POINTS

Refineries are an essential part of the oil and gas industry, responsible for converting crude oil into useful products such as gasoline, diesel, and jet fuel.

Building and running a refinery is a complex undertaking that requires careful planning, design, construction, operation, and maintenance.

Important factors to consider when planning a refinery include environmental impact assessments, regulatory requirements, and the selection of the appropriate refinery type and design.

During construction and commissioning, it is critical to ensure that the refinery is built to the required specifications, including proper installation of process equipment, instrumentation, electrical and control systems.

Operating a refinery requires monitoring and controlling the refining processes, troubleshooting and problem-solving, and implementing preventive and predictive maintenance strategies.

Refineries must comply with regulatory requirements and maintain high product quality standards through testing, inspection, and quality control measures.

Understanding the economics and finances of refinery operations, including cost estimation, profitability analysis, and risk management, is essential for long-term success.

Future trends and developments in the refining industry include the adoption of emerging technologies, renewable energy sources, and increased emphasis on sustainability and environmental considerations.

THE IMPORTANCE OF REFINING IN THE OIL AND GAS INDUSTRY

The refining of crude oil into useful products is a critical aspect of the oil and gas industry. Crude oil is a complex mixture of hydrocarbons, and refining involves breaking down these hydrocarbons into smaller molecules to produce various products such as gasoline, diesel, and jet fuel.

Without refineries, crude oil would be of little use, and the oil and gas industry would be unable to meet the demand for the numerous products that rely on refined oil. In addition to fuel products, refineries also produce other essential products such as lubricants, chemicals, and asphalt.

Refineries play a critical role in meeting the energy needs of individuals, businesses, and industries worldwide. They are an essential link in the oil and gas supply chain, providing the products necessary for transportation, manufacturing, and numerous other applications. In summary, refineries are crucial for the functioning of the oil and gas industry and the global economy as a whole.

THE POTENTIAL BENEFITS OF BUILDING AND RUNNING A REFINERY

Building and running a refinery can bring numerous potential benefits, including:

Increased revenue: Refineries are significant sources of revenue for their owners and operators, generating income from the sale of refined products.

Job creation: Refineries employ large numbers of people, creating job opportunities for engineers, technicians, operators, and administrative staff.

Local economic development: Refineries can drive local economic development, attracting other businesses to the area and providing support for local communities.

Energy independence: By producing refined products locally, countries can reduce their dependence on foreign oil and increase their energy independence.

Strategic importance: Refineries are often considered strategically important assets, as they can be used to support national security objectives and provide critical products during times of crisis.

Environmental benefits: Newer refineries often incorporate advanced technologies that reduce environmental impacts, such as emissions of greenhouse gases and other pollutants.

Overall, building and running a refinery can bring significant benefits, both for the operators and for the communities and economies in which they are located. However, it is important to recognize that refineries also come with potential risks and challenges, including environmental impacts, safety hazards, and economic uncertainties. Proper planning, design, and management are crucial to ensure that refineries are operated safely, efficiently, and in an environmentally responsible manner.

Final thoughts and recommendations

In conclusion, building and running a refinery can be a complex and challenging endeavor, but with proper planning, construction, operation, and maintenance, it can be a lucrative and rewarding venture. Refineries play a crucial role in the oil and gas industry by converting crude oil into valuable products such as gasoline, diesel, and jet fuel, among others.

The importance of complying with environmental regulations and maintaining safety and security cannot be overemphasized. Therefore, it is critical to conduct thorough environmental impact assessments and obtain necessary regulatory approvals before construction begins. Also, developing and implementing effective safety and security protocols is vital to protecting workers, the facility, and the surrounding environment.

Efficient operations, product quality control, and effective distribution are critical factors for the profitability and success of a refinery. Constant monitoring, troubleshooting, and maintenance are necessary to prevent downtime and ensure the refinery operates smoothly.

The future of the refining industry is exciting, with emerging technologies such as digitalization, automation, and renewable energy offering new opportunities and challenges. Refinery owners and operators must stay informed and adapt to these changes to remain competitive and sustainable.

In conclusion, building and running a refinery requires significant investment, technical expertise, and continuous effort. However, if done correctly, it can be a profitable and rewarding venture that contributes to economic development and energy security.

Printed in Poland
by Amazon Fulfillment
Poland Sp. z o.o., Wrocław
16 June 2023

bb977373-bfc9-4586-be7f-a627983b202eR01